Explore the Outdoors

Camping

Have Fun, Be Smart

by Jacqueline Ching

Rosen Publishing Group, Inc.
New York

For my beloved husband, Prentis. And for Poder and Pliny.

Published in 2000 by The Rosen Publishing Group, Inc.
29 East 21st Street, New York, NY 10010

Copyright © 2000 by The Rosen Publishing Group, Inc.

First Edition

Ching, Jacqueline.
    Camping : have fun, be smart / by Jacqueline Ching.
      p.   cm. — (Explore the outdoors)
    Includes bibliographical references and index.
    Summary: Describes the benefits of camping, as well as how to plan a trip, what gear to take, how to provide for safety, and how to protect the environment.
    ISBN 0-8239-3173-0
    1. Camping—Juvenile literature. [1. Camping.] I. Title. II. Series.
GV191.7 .C55 2000
796.54—dc21   99-055419
                                                                      CIP
                                                                      AC

Manufactured in the United States of America

Contents

Introduction: Camping Is for Everyone

Imagine falling asleep under a canopy of glittering stars, then waking to watch the sun's rays rise over the mountain crests from your cozy sleeping bag. In 1998, 29 million American adults visited a U.S. national park, many of them to camp. What makes people fall in love with outdoor living? Some people say it's the physical challenge of "roughing it." Others go in search of wildlife, scenery, or plain old-fashioned adventure. One thing is certain: with so many ways to camp and so many kinds of campgrounds, camping is for everyone. Public campgrounds are all around you—in national parks, forests, recreation areas, and state and county parks.

If you've never camped before, you may have some doubts about starting now. Maybe you don't think of yourself as an outdoorsy person. Maybe you're concerned that it's too expensive. Well, you don't need previous outdoor experience to camp, nor do you have to be an athlete. You don't need a lot of money to camp either. The most important things to keep in mind when camping are to stay safe and to have fun. Camping will expose you to many new experiences. Learn how to approach these experiences the correct way to avoid getting hurt and enjoy an adventure of a lifetime.

Today, many travelers also use outfitters or guides to see the great outdoors. This can be a wonderful, safe way to try new

A morning view of nature is breathtaking.

outdoor sports, such as rock climbing, caving, fishing, or kayaking. Outfitters run trips of different lengths in different parts of the United States and Canada and even the rest of the world. These trips range from easy to strenuous.

Organizations dedicated to outdoor conservation and recreation also offer trips for families and people with varying levels of outdoor experience. These groups, such as the Sierra Club and the Appalachian Mountain Club, promote environmentally conscious use and protection of natural treasures. Like outfitters, they offer a safe way to try new outdoor activities at carefully selected destinations. However, if you're new to camping, you may want to try a short trip on your own before signing up for an expensive guided tour.

You can camp in many different ways in countless locations. No matter what type of trip you decide on, you're bound to have an amazing adventure.

1 Setting Off

A successful camping trip means different things to different people. Some people feel that they have to really rough it. Others want to bring along the comforts of home. Of course, camping implies a certain amount of roughing it, but to what extent depends on you. Decide what you want and begin to make a plan.

Initial Planning

For the best camping experience, start your trip at home. You will need to make some decisions. What kind of food will you bring? What kind of clothes? Equipment? What about shelter?

Before you decide on these things, ask yourself what kind of camping experience you hope to have. Will you have a car nearby? What is the length of your trip? Will you stay at a base camp or move to different sites? How many days will you stay at each site? How long does it take to get to each location? What will the weather be like?

Decide how long to camp. You may be content to spend a weekend away from beds and microwaves, but not a week. If it is solitude you seek, be aware of when and where you are most likely to run into crowds. For example, you can expect a crowd in the Great Smoky Mountains National Park during the peak of

Locating yourself with a map and compass is a confidence-building skill.

autumn colors. If you are traveling with friends, discuss everyone's expectations beforehand. Campers who expect relax-
ation and contemplation may not mix well with campers
intent on breaking hiking records. Make time for everyone to
explore on his or her own.

    For your first few trips, practice your camping skills
closer to home and in well-traveled areas. It takes years to
become an expert who knows by instinct how to keep safe in
the wilderness.

    An important part of your plan is weather. You can
start by choosing a season when your tent is least likely to be
flooded by rain, but you should also keep track of weather
systems immediately before your trip. Always be prepared for
the unexpected.

The local forest ranger can help make your trip safer.

As you complete your initial plan, contact park officials at your destination. They will be able to advise you on making other preparations. They can inform you about unseasonable weather, bear warnings, availability of campsites, need for reservations, fees, available activities, rules, and regulations. Today, most campgrounds have e-mail addresses and Web sites where you can seek information.

Your Budget

Your initial plan should include a budget. How much money do you intend to spend? If money is tight, don't go too far into the wilderness. The farther out you go, the more specialized the equipment you will need, which can be expensive. Also, the longer your trip, the more supplies and equipment you will have to bring. Ask about camping fees at your destination. And don't forget to figure in your travel costs (such as gasoline and car parking fees).

Choosing a Campground

There are more kinds of campgrounds than you can imagine. The terrain in a coastal area will differ greatly from an alpine highland. You will need to do some research before choosing a site.

Be aware of the campground's geography and native plants and animals. Find out in advance if your campground's terrain is near a body of water, thickly forested, or steep and mountainous. Your research should also help you stay far

Modern tents are designed for different climates.

away from thick woods, deep grass, and stagnant ponds; these places strongly attract insects. Before any trip, ask local park officials about conditions at your prospective campsite. The information they give you will help you to organize your clothing, gear, and first-aid kit. For instance, if you're going to snake country, you may want to pack a snakebite kit. Also, it's easier to camp at established campgrounds. Most of them have basic amenities, such as safe water supplies, showers, and bathrooms.

Outdoor Activities

You can also choose a campground based on the activities it offers. Is there fishing? Canoeing? Kayaking? Hiking? Climbing? Remember that for certain activities you will need

Getting lost can be a stressful experience.

special equipment and supplies, such as a fishing rod. You may also need special licenses.

Permits

Camping permits enable park officials to keep track of the number of visitors, in case of emergency, and to control the use of park facilities. As soon as you choose a destination, apply for the necessary permits. You may be able to get a permit when you arrive, you may need one in advance, or you may not need one at all. Rules differ from place to place.

A Final Word

Although you're smart to have a plan, remember that you can't plan everything. You may not have a choice where you camp. The weather may change drastically. Some of your experience will depend on luck; it will also depend on your attitude and creativity. You're on an adventure, and the most important thing you can bring with you is your ability to improvise.

2 What to Wear

The first rule of packing for a camping trip: pack smart. Start by making a list of what to bring. You'll want to pack clothes that are not too bulky or too heavy to carry. You can buy specialized outdoor wear at outdoor suppliers, but before you get a whole new wardrobe, check your closet.

Basic Good Sense

When you pack to go camping, the most important question is: What will the temperature and weather be? Do you expect rain? Heat?

Don't carry more weight than you can handle.

Morning frost? Although you can listen to the weather forecast before your departure and predict the weather to some degree, you could get caught in an unexpected rain shower or heat wave. Temperatures at some campsites can range from 25 to 90 degrees Fahrenheit in a day even in the middle of summer. Temperatures can drop dramatically after nightfall. Make sure you're prepared for changes in weather.

If you plan on being outdoors for a long time, then the expense of buying outdoor wear makes sense. However, if you're a beginning camper, stick with the versatile classics. In mild weather, clothes made of cotton, like T-shirts and jeans, work well. They are comfortable and lightweight. You can also layer several T-shirts as needed. However, because cotton absorbs moisture, it doesn't work in wet or cold weather. Therefore, most outdoor clothing is made from synthetic fabrics.

Sweats are useful, too. You can sleep in them, and they're very warm. If possible, choose sweats that are 50 percent acrylic. They cost less, weigh less, and dry more quickly than 100 percent cotton clothing.

Layering

Since there are no guarantees when it comes to weather, the all-purpose solution is to layer your clothes. Layering gives you maximum flexibility.

● For the inner layer, choose wool or synthetic fabrics. Long underwear made of polyester or polypropylene may be your best buy. It keeps moisture away from the body. In summer, it keeps you cool and dry even when you sweat, and in winter it provides added insulation.

● The middle layer should insulate you. Choose a fleece jacket or wool sweater. Fleece is lighter and absorbs less moisture than wool.

● The outer layer protects against weather. Choose a water-proof windbreaker. This inexpensive item is lightweight and warm and can also protect you from rain. In the mountains, weather is even more unpredictable. It is essential that you bring some kind of rainwear. Wet skin and clothing, plus low temperatures and wind, can lead to hypothermia, a serious illness caused by exposure to excessive cold.

Because of the increasing popularity of outdoor activities, there are more choices in outerwear than ever. Today's parkas and jackets combine natural and synthetic fabrics and offer warmth without additional weight or bulk, which makes them easier to carry. A down vest is another useful item of clothing. People allergic to down can find synthetic alternatives. In winter, bring a parka or a jacket. In summer, pack your shorts. And, of course, in any season, don't forget a supply of clean socks and underwear.

When you are exposed to the elements, the key to keeping warm is to conserve your body's heat. You may have heard the bit of old wisdom: "If your feet are cold, put on a hat." This is because you lose a lot of body heat from your head. Hats come in wool, fleece, or acrylic. Don't leave your hat at home!

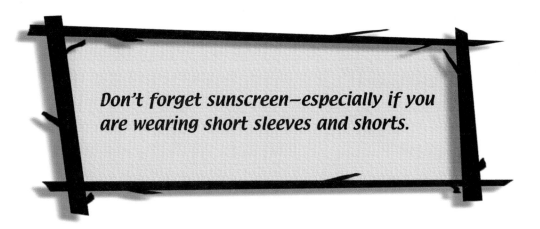

Don't forget sunscreen—especially if you are wearing short sleeves and shorts.

For the Feet

Expect a lot of walking when you go camping. You may need to do a bit of hiking to reach the best vistas. Therefore, you can do yourself no bigger favor than to invest in good socks. They stand between you and pain. Socks made for walking and hiking come in natural and synthetic blends. They give your feet support, protect your tendons, and absorb shock. They also keep your feet warm or cool, and above all, dry.

Equally important is a good shoe. If you are only planning short hikes on gentle trails, a good running shoe will do very nicely. Make sure to choose shoes that give plenty of support and absorb a lot of shock. In warmer weather, or if you are planning water activities, it's a good idea to bring waterproof sandals.

Hiking boots are preferable for longer hikes because they are sturdier, give you ankle support, and absorb shock. If you go shopping for boots, make certain that they fit properly. Bring the socks you plan on using for hiking, and try on the boots with the socks. Walk down an incline and see if your heel stays in place. There should be no slippage when you are hiking downhill in your expensive boots.

Good hiking shoes are essential.

3 Essential Gear

A warm, cozy tent at night makes all the difference.

It's your first night camping, and you wake up before sunrise. The truth is, you never really got to sleep. Your teeth are chattering, and your back aches from the pebbles under your sleeping bag. You decide to get up and make hot coffee. You might as well, it's morning anyway. But it's still dark out, and you didn't pack a flashlight, and in the dark you can't find the matches you brought.

Does this sound like a camper's worst nightmare? For some, it's real life. Don't end up cold and stranded in the dark, dying for a cup of coffee. Pack the essentials.

Backpacks—A Portable Home

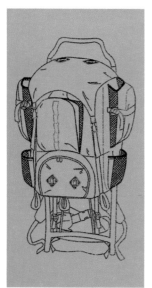

Your backpack is your portable home. It will carry everything you need. Make certain everything fits in the backpack, and that the pack fits well on you.

Cheaper backpacks come one-size-fits-all. They are usually adequate for short trips. If you spend more money, you can get one that is adjustable. Look for a good hip belt, which can take the pressure off your neck and shoulders.

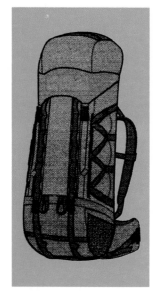

There are two basic styles of backpack: external frame and internal frame. External frame backpacks have a metal frame attached to the outside of the pack to support it. Frames are made of aluminum or nylon. These packs are great for general backpacking, especially for heavy loads. A good external-frame backpack usually costs between $100 and $200. They are also available for about $50, but beware of cheaply designed frames that come apart under a heavy load.

The internal-frame backpack is less bulky and gives you more freedom of

Modern pack frames distribute weight properly.

movement. Mountaineers, skiers, and climbers prefer this pack because it tends to balance more easily. But beware: This snugly fitting pack will leave you perspiring in warm temperatures.

Day Packs

Day packs are smaller then backpacks. As with full-size backpacks, the key to the day pack is support. Look for a curve on the back of the pack matching the curve of your spine. Again, choose one with a good hip belt.

Day packs come with a variety of features. You will probably find it useful to have a couple of outside pockets (for pocketknives, water bottles, snacks) and maybe an ax loop, on which to hang additional items.

Picking a Tent

A tent is a big purchase, but the right one can last a lifetime. It's also an important purchase if you want to get a good night's sleep.

The price of tents varies widely. The major differences between tents are the materials (zippers, seam sealings, pole systems) and the stitching. More expensive tents are double stitched, which is very labor intensive. Some tents are also waterproof, but others are merely water resistant. When it comes to poles, aluminum alloy poles are considered the best in terms of weight and durability.

A good night's sleep in the outdoors can be refreshing.

Tents are designed with different camping conditions and seasons in mind. A summer tent is light and lets in a lot of air. It may have features such as mesh windows and a mesh roof for viewing the night sky and keeping out mosquitoes. A three-season tent makes sense if you plan on doing a lot of camping. It works well in mild weather but can also handle heavy rainstorms. An all-season tent gives extra protection against sharp winds, snow, or sleet. It also weighs two to four pounds more than the others. If you expect to do a lot of backpacking or hiking, you may decide to sacrifice comfort for weight. Generally, the tougher tents will weigh more.

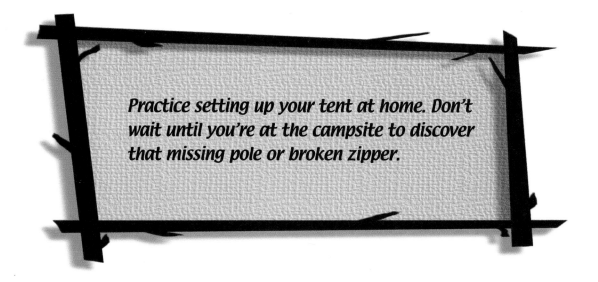

Practice setting up your tent at home. Don't wait until you're at the campsite to discover that missing pole or broken zipper.

What About a Tarp?

A tarp is a useful, but optional, item. It provides shade on hot days and a roof when it rains. Consider this, too: After collecting your firewood, you may need something to protect it from rain and moisture. Some tarps come with poles; others

Tent Shapes

SHAPE	PROS	CONS
A-Frame Tent	Tent will withstand wind and rain. Simple design.	Cramped interior. Some require stakes; others are freestanding.

SHAPE	PROS	CONS
Dome Tent	Good three-season tent. Upright walls leave lots of room.	Heavy to carry. May blow away if not properly staked.

SHAPE	PROS	CONS
Hoop Tent	Light and easy to set up. High ceilings.	Not for heavy winds or storms.

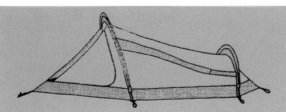

SHAPE	PROS	CONS
Pyramid Tent	Light and easy to set up.	No built-in floor means no protection from water or bugs.

are held aloft by ropes tied to trees. To prevent the tarp from becoming a basin of water when it rains, you must somehow elevate its center. You can purchase an aluminum center pole or hang your tarp over a rope so the rainwater runs off.

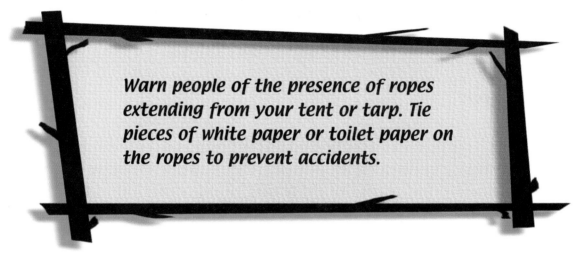

Warn people of the presence of ropes extending from your tent or tarp. Tie pieces of white paper or toilet paper on the ropes to prevent accidents.

Sleeping Bags: The Options

Because camping usually means sleeping outdoors, the most important item to bring is your sleeping bag. When you buy your sleeping bag, ask yourself how much camping you plan to do. If you camp a lot, invest in a higher-quality bag. If you only camp now and then, such an expense may not be worthwhile. In general, a three-season bag will probably be the best buy. A good rule of thumb is to think of the coldest temperatures you will be sleeping in. You can always leave your bag unzipped if you get too hot. There's not much you can do if you're too cold.

You can choose your sleeping bag based on its temperature or comfort rating. A summer fair-weather bag has a minimum rating of between 40 and 50 degrees Fahrenheit. This means it can keep you snug when it's 40 to 50 degrees Fahrenheit outside. For cooler weather, choose one that has a

Your tent should be roomy enough for everyone to sleep comfortably.

minimum rating of between 20 and 25 degrees Fahrenheit, or, for winter camping, a minimum rating of 10 degrees Fahrenheit or lower. Keep in mind, however, that the manufacturers rate their own products and that there is no universal rating system for bags.

Sleeping bags are filled with either down or synthetic materials. There are pros and cons to both. Down bags are light, warm, and compressible. Goose down is the best insulator. However, a good down bag can be very expensive. Also, if your bag should get wet, a synthetic bag will keep you warmer than a down bag.

Synthetic bags have improved greatly and are usually far cheaper than down bags. In weight and compression, however, they still can't beat down bags. A down bag can weigh three pounds, whereas a synthetic bag with the same insulating power weighs two or three pounds more. Down bags compress about 25 percent smaller, too. If you do choose a synthetic bag, don't store it compacted. Doing so causes the fibers to break down and your bag to lose its insulation.

Another consideration when choosing a sleeping bag is its size and shape. You'll want enough room to stretch out but not too much room for air. Your body has to heat that extra space. Before buying a sleeping bag, try it on for size. Roll around in it and feel the fit. The basic shapes are mummy (a tight-fitting bag with hood), semi-mummy (like the mummy but with a looser fit), and rectangular (open at the top and thus less heat-efficient).

Lastly, check the zipper before you buy your sleeping bag. Compare the zipper quality of several bags.

Sleeping Pads

Traditionally, Native Americans and pioneers laid down pine needles, grass, dry leaves, or straw for bedding. A more practical choice is available to today's campers: the sleeping pad. With such a pad, the rocks or roots underneath you won't be as noticeable. The sleeping pad will also keep you warmer.

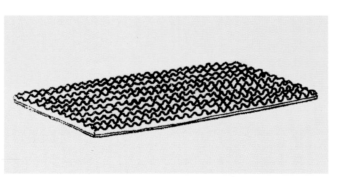

A foam sleeping pad

You can buy foam pads or air mattresses to use as sleeping pads, but old sleeping bags or extra blankets will do the trick, too. As always, you have to factor in bulkiness and weight when packing these extra items.

Other Stuff You'll Need

You won't be waking up to the comforts of modern plumbing, so decide what you will need to keep clean. Don't forget your toiletries: toothbrush and toothpaste, towel, lip balm and sunscreen, wet wipes, and toilet paper. There may be other things you will need, such as sanitary napkins or tampons.

You won't want to be without a flashlight. Many campers prefer a miner's light, which is worn on the head, to free up your hands for other tasks. Remember to bring extra batteries.

You also won't want to go hungry. It takes a lot of skill to build a fire without a lighter or matches, so make sure to bring them. Keep waterproof matches in a waterproof container. A butane lighter dries easily and lights repeatedly.

A fully stocked first-aid kit is essential.

A knife will come in handy for cooking, setting up tents and tarps, and emergencies. In addition to a sturdy knife, you may want to pack a multiuse camp tool.

Finally, don't forget a compass and a map. You can pack them, but do you know how to use them? Make sure you do; it's not as easy as you may think.

4 Establishing Camp

If you plan to camp during peak season, you must plan ahead. In summer, don't expect to camp at popular destinations, such as Yellowstone or Yosemite, without reserving a campsite. Many campgrounds also have sites available on a first-come, first-served basis. Contact your local, county, or state parks and recreation department to find out whether to make reservations or arrive early and take your chances.

Modern dome tents can withstand the elements well.

At any park, make the visitor center your first stop. There you will find information on attractions, facilities, and activities. Some parks offer scenic drives, historic tours, cruises, and ranger-guided programs. The park staff will also answer questions about accommodations, services, and special attractions.

Choosing a Campsite

At your destination, park officials may direct you to where you are allowed to camp. However, you still have to pick the site to pitch your tent and build a fire. You should pick a place where there is an existing fire ring or fire pit. Doing so will minimize your impact on the environment.

Follow these guidelines when choosing a campsite:
- Don't camp under snags, or dead trees, which can fall.
- Don't camp near gullies, overhanging rocks, and bear trails.
- Don't camp under a lone tree, in case of a lightning storm.
- Keep to higher ground and avoid areas that turn into swamps after rain.
- Find a good exposure. You'll want sun in the morning for warmth and shade in the afternoon.
- Make sure plenty of firewood is nearby.
- Camp away from game trails so you don't disturb animals.

Take advantage of daylight to check around your campsite for dangerous ditches, poison ivy or poison oak, beehives, and anything else that may result in a hazardous encounter in the dark.

Before pitching your tent, choose a level place and clear away all debris. You'll sleep better with fewer rocks and twigs under the tent. Pitch your tent away from the fire. Don't pitch

Thoroughly quench your campfire before you go to sleep.

your tent on ground foliage. You have your sleeping pad for comfort and warmth.

Fire Safety

You don't want to be responsible for burning down the forest. Follow fire-building safety guidelines and be proactive in protecting the environment. You can start by making a small fire, so that you burn only the wood you need. Don't burn live wood. Besides, collecting fallen branches is part of the fun.

Although fire regulations are often posted in campgrounds or at trailheads, you should always ask park officials about current conditions. In the summer or in a drought, open fires are prohibited, but you will still be able to use your pack stove or a pit fireplace, which can be found in certain campgrounds. You may be required to have a shovel and a bucket of water near the fire. Sometimes you need a fire permit.

You can get up-to-date information by calling any local office of the U.S. Forest Service, U.S. Bureau of Land Management, National Park Service, or state forestry department. It's important to learn the regulations before you strike that match.

How to Build a Fire

Make sure your fire ring sits about six-feet clear of any flammable materials, such as dried twigs, grass, or overhanging branches. There should be a circle of rocks around the ring to keep the wind from blowing out your fire.

Make sure to gather enough firewood first. You will need small, dry twigs, as well as larger sticks of wood. Build a tepee-shaped structure in the middle of the fire ring. Take your butane lighter or matches and light the small twigs. As they catch, start to feed larger sticks to the flames.

If you are cooking with coals, you should dig a trench near the fire circle to store the coals. From the trench, you can easily shovel the coals into the fire.

Food, Food, and More Food

Being outdoors takes a lot of energy. Carrying a thirty-pound pack over long trails can really create an appetite. A good rule of thumb is to carry two pounds of food (excluding packaging) per day per person. Look for food that will keep your energy up and that is lightweight, easy to prepare, and won't spoil easily. Make sure any perishable food, like milk, butter, and mayonnaise, are kept cool to keep them fresh.

A great idea is to plan all your cooked meals in advance. Measure all the ingredients and place them into separate bags. Prepare some fresh vegetables, like carrots and celery, in bags, too. Fattening foods that you avoid at home, like peanut

A good breakfast lifts the spirits!

butter sandwiches or dried salami, are perfect for camping. You can indulge in eggs and bacon for breakfast. You'll need lots of calories to enjoy outdoor activities. Don't skimp on proteins or fat, the body's fuel.

Bring along lots of snacks. Nuts are high in energy. Fresh fruit, like apples and oranges, are another great snack, but they can get heavy if you bring too many. Don't forget trail mix and granola bars.

For longer trips, freeze-dried food is the most practical in terms of weight and ease of preparation. It also offers variety, from macaroni and cheese to noodle and rice dishes. On the other hand, freeze-dried food requires water. One meal might require two and a half cups of boiling water to cook. Consider your water sources before packing. You can supplement freeze-dried foods with crackers, cereals, and dried soups.

If you are planning to cook, don't forget utensils and cooking staples, such as oil, flour, and butter. At a minimum, you will need a pot (for soups, hot drinks, and treating water), a frying pan, fire grill, cooking spoon, spatula, can opener, pot holders, cutlery, and dishes.

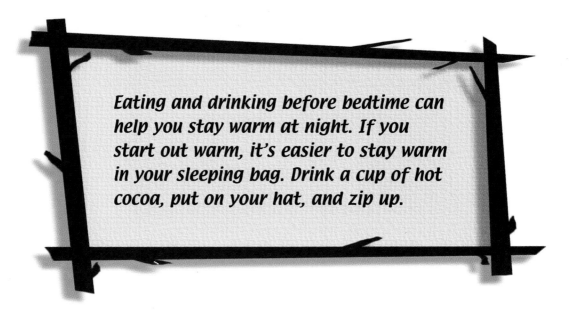

Eating and drinking before bedtime can help you stay warm at night. If you start out warm, it's easier to stay warm in your sleeping bag. Drink a cup of hot cocoa, put on your hat, and zip up.

A Warning About Water

The water around organized campgrounds is usually treated to be safe, but that's not true in the wilderness. Unfortunately, most natural water sources today contain either biological or chemical contaminants. The simple rule is: Don't drink untreated water unless it's an emergency.

This warning is a very serious one. Untreated water may contain bacteria such as E. coli, salmonella, and cholera. Bacteria, viruses, and parasites can leave you with diarrhea, vomiting, or worse. These biological contaminants can also cause typhoid, strep throat, dysentery, and other diseases.

Ways to Treat Water

With Iodine

Iodine, if used correctly, will kill most waterborne organisms, like those at right. It comes in tablet, crystal, and liquid form. Iodine is even effective against giardia, a parasite that causes stomach cramps, diarrhea, and vomiting. In order for iodine to kill giardia, the water has to be at least 69 degrees Fahrenheit.

After adding iodine, wait at least thirty minutes before drinking the water. For better-tasting water, add neutralizing tablets and shake the water. Drink mixes will also cover the taste of the iodine.

By Boiling

Bringing water to a boil can kill all parasites and bacteria. To be safe, boil water for three to five minutes.

By Filtration

Portable lightweight water filters will strain out most bacteria, viruses, and parasites. Water filters can weigh as little as one pound but can be fairly expensive. Remember to bring an extra filter for trips longer than one night.

Water filtration system

33

None of these methods is 100 percent effective, so you may want to combine two of them for extra insurance. For example, iodine alone is ineffective against the parasite cryptosporidium, which produces fever, vomiting, fatigue, and diarrhea. Water filters alone cannot strain away the tiniest of organisms. These need to be killed by boiling the water or by adding iodine. Some water filters have built-in iodine chambers to guarantee full protection. Whether you boil or filter your water, take this added step to avoid animal contamination: Go upstream from where you find evidence of animals, such as a beaver dam, to draw your water. When it comes to your drinking water, don't take any chances.

5 Animals and Plants

Camping gives you a chance to learn more about nature. While you're exploring, it is your responsibility to keep your distance from wild animals and to learn not to antagonize them. If you follow trail etiquette, you will protect yourself from danger.

Although it's safer to explore the wild in a group than to do so alone, keep your group small. That way, it's easier to avoid disturbing animals and plants. If there is a trail, stay on it. If you need to go off the trail, step gently around delicate turf.

A well-marked trail makes hiking easier.

Singing or whistling as you walk along a trail warns animals of your approach and prevents them from being startled. Most bears, for instance, will go away when they detect your presence. When it comes to wild animals, simply stay out of their way. They are usually more afraid of you than you are of them.

Although viewing wildlife is an exciting part of camping, it should be done from a safe distance. Use binoculars or a telephoto lens. You are more likely to spot wildlife if you walk slowly and stop occasionally to look around. Bring a good field guide from the library, or call your state wildlife office for information on specific animals you want to see. The more you know about wildlife, the better you can protect it and yourself from mutual harm.

You can visit these Web sites for more information on wildlife:
- National Wildlife Federation—http://www.nwf.org
- National Audubon Society—http://www.audubon.org
- Nature Conservancy—http://www.tnc.org
- National Resources Defense Council—http://www.nrdc.org
- The Wilderness Society—http://www.wilderness.org

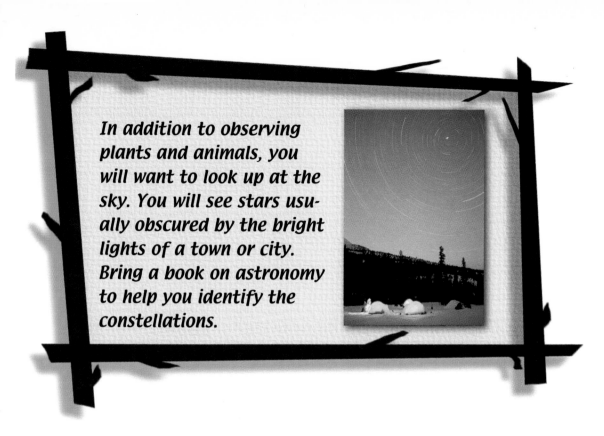

In addition to observing plants and animals, you will want to look up at the sky. You will see stars usually obscured by the bright lights of a town or city. Bring a book on astronomy to help you identify the constellations.

Big, Bad Bears

There are about 625,000 bears in North America. In the wilderness, bears tend to keep their distance. In U.S. national parks, however, bears are more accustomed to human company and may be bolder. Don't ever feed a bear, especially if it is a cub. You may provoke its mother's anger.

Don't give a bear reason to rob your camp. Odors, even the ones coming from your cooler, attract bears. Keep your food and cooking items locked up tightly or stored high in a tree sling. Make sure your food is at least eight feet off the ground and four feet away from the nearest weight-bearing branch. Never keep food in your tent. In the dark, when bears are most active, use a flashlight to warn them of your presence. By keeping bears away from your camp, you are also keeping it safe for future campers.

Black bears outnumber grizzly bears, which are an

Observing wild animals is a rare treat, but stay away!

endangered species. However, you are just as likely to encounter a grizzly as a black bear, because grizzlies are more aggressive. Most bears attack when they are startled. If you should have such an encounter, back up slowly (never run) while singing or talking. Don't be threatening and always give the bear an escape route. Avoid eye contact.

If you are charged by a bear, remember that playing dead works with a grizzly but not with a black bear. If a black bear charges you, shout and kick. If you climb up a tree, make sure you can get higher than twelve feet. Small grizzlies and black bears can climb trees, too.

If you see bear warnings posted on trails, contact park staff for details. It means that bear activity is greater than normal, and you may have to take extra precautions by avoiding natural bear foods such as berries, nuts, fish, and animal flesh.

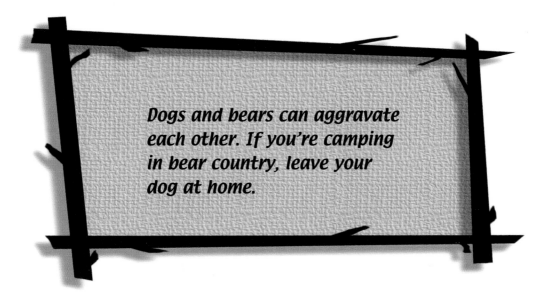

Dogs and bears can aggravate each other. If you're camping in bear country, leave your dog at home.

Treating Animal Bites

If someone is bitten by a bear or other animal, try to stop any heavy bleeding. If there is no bleeding, wash the wound thoroughly with water and if possible with soap. Apply a clean dressing to the wound. Treat the victim for shock. Get medical help as soon as possible to prevent infection. Symptoms of infection are pain and tenderness, redness, heat, swelling, pus, and red streaks around the wound. Try to identify the specific animal that bit the person.

Staying Safe from Snakes

Most people don't take precautions against snakebites very seriously. However, it's important to be very careful when outdoors, particularly if you're camping somewhere with a large snake population or native, poisonous snakes. In snake country, never reach into a hole or bush where your vision is obscured. Never sit down without inspecting the area around you. Be careful when stepping over logs. Walk slowly so as not to startle a snake, and avoid walking at night, when snakes are most active.

Don't advance upon or agitate a snake.

Treating Snakebites

The best thing to do if bitten by a snake is to get professional medical help as soon as possible. Wash the wound and immobilize the injured area, keeping it lower than the heart, if possible. Take an antihistamine to control the reaction to the venom. Keep very still or walk very slowly to keep your pulse down and to slow your blood flow.

Contrary to popular belief, you should not apply ice, cut the wound, or use a tourniquet. Although the effectiveness of a snakebite kit is in debate, it may help you temporarily. Encourage bleeding from the wound and try suctioning it. Using your mouth to suction should always be your last resort. If possible, note the snake's markings to help identify it.

Insects and Ticks

Woods are prime tick territory, and places near water are great for mosquitoes (like the one on the next page). There are also gnats, ants, yellow jackets, wasps, and a host of other residents of the outdoors. So, unless you're traveling in the fall or winter, pack protection.

Mainstream insect repellents use DEET, which is effective but toxic. Use it sparingly and keep it away from hands, eyes, mouth, and open wounds. Check the product. A 30 percent DEET concentration is enough to do the job. There are alternatives to using a DEET product, but their effectiveness may vary greatly. In addition to natural insect repellent products, you can use mosquito coils and citronella candles.

You can also try spraying your clothes with the DEET product before spraying yourself. Spray your tent and then allow it to air out. Be careful not to spray any food supplies or cooking utensils.

Mosquitos and other insects can make your life miserable.

Expert campers are more wary of ticks than of any other animal. Tick bites can easily get infected and, even worse, can cause Lyme disease. To avoid ticks, take the precaution of wearing long pants and high socks, especially in springtime. Spray insect repellent on your legs, too. It's also a good idea to check your legs for ticks every hour or two if you're walking through bushes.

Treating Insect Bites and Stings

If you are stung by an insect, try to kill it so you can identify it. Some home remedies for insect bites are ice, household ammonia, meat tenderizer, and mud. Insect bites are life-threatening to those who have a severe allergy to the venom. The most common insect-bite allergy is to the bee sting. If you are stung by a bee, remove the stinger as quickly as possible.

If the victim is allergic to the sting, and particularly if he or she has been stung a number of times, seek medical help immediately. Symptoms of an allergic reaction include swelling of the throat, dizziness, redness or discoloration around the bite, itching, hives, and difficulty breathing.

Poisonous Plants

The most important rule to remember about plants in the wild: Don't eat anything. Never eat any plants that you cannot identify. This includes leaves, berries, stems, mushrooms, and all other plant parts. Some poisonous plants closely resemble other, safe plants. If in any doubt at all, don't eat it.

Learn to recognize poison ivy, poison sumac, and poison oak. These are the most common poisonous plants you'll see when camping. Contact with them can cause an allergic reaction on the skin that results in itchy red rashes and sometimes blisters. Luckily, the rash is not contagious and goes away in about two weeks. Scratching will spread infection.

Treating Poison Ivy, Sumac, and Oak

If you come into contact with poison ivy (pictured above), poison sumac, or poison oak, wash the area thoroughly with strong soap, then apply calamine lotion. Running hot water on it can alleviate the itching. Remove and wash any clothing that may have come in contact with the plant oils.

6 Emergencies

Here's the best camping advice you are going to get anywhere, anytime: Before your trip, take a course in basic first aid. These may be the best few hours you'll ever spend. You really can save a life.

Many local groups offer basic first-aid courses. The American Red Cross recommends its course, First Aid Responding to Emergencies, for campers. You must take CPR as a prerequisite. This course covers severe bleeding, internal bleeding, shock, muscle and skeletal injuries, diagnoses of illness, how to move victims, and what to do if help can't get to you. Call your local American Red Cross for more information. First aid is important for anyone to know, but it is essential for campers.

Before leaving on your trip, you must also give trusted friends and family members your itinerary. Give them details about where you are camping, including the phone numbers of your cell phone or pager (if you have one) and of the campground office and the nearest forest service office.

Be aware that conditions differ from one campground to another. Although you may have camped before, don't take things for granted. Aside from bears, snakes, poison ivy, and polluted water, the terrain itself can pose a hazard. Avoid taking unnecessary risks, such as walking on loose rocks and mud near

Pamphlets produced by the National Parks Service

slopes and cliffs, standing under dead trees and dead branches in a storm, and moving quickly through heavy brush. It is also a good idea to familiarize yourself with the terrain around your campsite before nightfall, taking note of any holes, ditches, or other potential hazards. In other words, pay attention to any new environment.

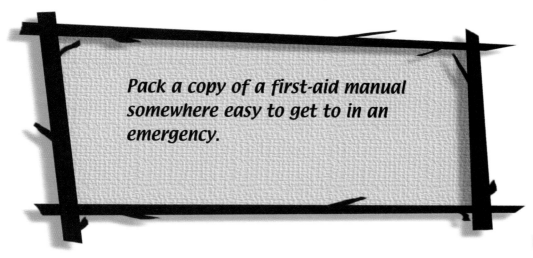

Pack a copy of a first-aid manual somewhere easy to get to in an emergency.

Shock

Shock is the failure of the cardiovascular system to keep enough blood circulating to the heart, lungs, and brain. Many injuries, infections, and illnesses can cause shock. Sometimes shock is the result of a severe allergic reaction. It is life-threatening if left untreated.

Immediately after an injury, observe the victim for symptoms of shock. These include confusion; very fast or very slow pulse rate; very fast or very slow breathing; shivering and weakness in the arms or legs; cool and moist skin; pale or bluish skin, lips, and fingernails; and enlarged pupils. If you anticipate that shock may follow an injury, take these first-aid measures:

- Maintain the victim's body temperature. If the victim is cold, wrap him or her in a blanket. If hot, keep him or her cool.
- Keep the victim lying down, comfortable, and calm. This improves circulation.
- If the victim is not suspected of having head, neck, or back injuries or leg fractures, elevate the legs.
- If you suspect head or neck injuries, keep the victim lying flat. If vomiting occurs, turn the victim on his or her side.
- If the victim has trouble breathing, move him or her into a semi-reclining position.

Bleeding

If someone is bleeding heavily, take first-aid measures to stop the bleeding, prevent infection, and prevent shock.

1. To control bleeding, apply direct pressure to the wound. Use a dressing, if available. Otherwise, a towel or piece of clothing will do. If the dressing becomes soaked with blood, always apply new dressings over old ones, so as not to disturb the wound.

2. Elevate the wound above the level of the heart and continue to apply direct pressure. Warning: Don't do this if you suspect there is a fracture.

3. Apply a bandage over the wound. Pressure should be used in applying the bandage. Warning: Check the pulse to make sure the bandage is not cutting circulation. A slow pulse rate or bluish fingertips or toes may be signs that the bandage is too tight.

Burns

Burns are most severe when located on the face, neck, hands, feet, and genitals, or spread over large parts of the body. Burns cause pain, infection, and shock.

First-Degree Burns

First-degree burns are the least severe type of burn. First-degree burns usually exhibit redness or discoloration, mild swelling, and pain. A sunburn is the most common first-degree burn. For treatment, soak the burn in or run it under cool water. Then apply moist dressings and bandage loosely.

Second- and Third-Degree Burns

Second-degree burns may be the most painful because although the burn is deeper, the nerve endings are still intact. With severe burns, don't break any blisters. Apply first-aid ointment and dry dressings, then bandage loosely. Treat the victim for shock and get medical help as soon as possible. Do not use ice or water, as these may increase the risk of shock.

Dehydration

Remember that water may not be readily available at your campsite. You must not drink from any natural water source without first treating the water. Dehydration occurs quickly, especially during strenuous activity at higher altitudes. Always carry at least a full bottle of consumable water.

Vomiting and diarrhea are not life-threatening until they cause dehydration. Even if someone has a problem taking in food and liquid, it is important that he or she take frequent sips of water to replace lost fluids. In cases of severe dehydration, get medical help as soon as possible.

Fractures and Sprains

Symptoms of fractures and sprains include pain, tenderness, swelling, bruising, a feeling of bones rubbing together, and an inability to move the injured body part.

Do the following to treat fractures and sprains:

- Control bleeding, if necessary.
- Tie splints to the affected area to prevent further movement, taking care not to cause additional pain to the victim.
- Apply a cold compress to reduce pain and swelling.
- Treat the victim for shock.
- Get medical help as soon as possible.

Hypothermia

Exposure to the severe cold, high winds, and dampness can cause this life-threatening condition. Look for symptoms such as shivering, dizziness, numbness, confusion, weakness, impaired judgment, impaired vision, and drowsiness. In its advanced stages, the victim will experience a loss of consciousness and decreased pulse and breathing rates, which can be fatal.

Cold weather can be dangerous.

For treatment, keep the victim warm and dry. Move him or her to a shelter and remove any wet clothing. Use sleeping bags and emergency blankets to make sure the person is well-insulated from the ground as well as from the wind. If the victim is fully conscious, give him or her warm liquids. Get medical help as soon as possible.

Heatstroke

Heatstroke is caused by a combination of high temperatures, sun, and strenuous exercise. Take immediate action. When a person has heatstroke, body temperature rises so high that brain damage and death can result unless the body is cooled quickly.

Symptoms of heatstroke include hot, red, and dry skin; small pupils; and very high body temperature. If you observe any of these symptoms, cool the victim as soon as possible, in any way possible. This means moving the person to a cool, shaded place; using a fan; applying a cool body wash with a sponge or wet towel; or putting him or her in a tub of cool water. Treat the person for shock. Get medical help as soon as possible. Do not give the person anything by mouth.

Always drink plenty of water when hiking in hot climates.

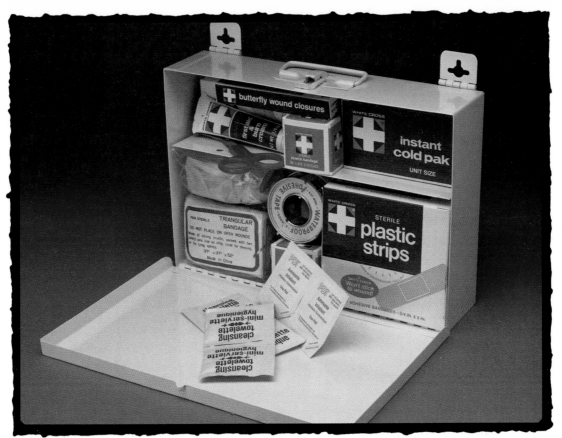

Simple first aid kits are inexpensive—and essential for campers.

First-Aid Kit: Don't Leave Home Without It

You can buy a prepackaged first-aid kit or assemble your own. It is not enough to pack a kit; you need to familiarize yourself with its contents and learn what to do in an emergency. If you don't learn about it in your basic first-aid course, seek out other sources of information, such as a course on wilderness first aid.

If you decide to buy a kit, you will discover that they range from inexpensive kits, which are good for minor injuries, to more expensive heavy-duty kits, which contain supplies for treating blisters, wounds, burns, trauma, and handling infectious materials.

How old is your first-aid kit? Check it periodically to restock items that have been used and to replace expired medications.

Even on marked trails, a map is helpful.

Getting Lost

Although no one expects to get lost, you can make sure that if you do, you'll be as comfortable as possible. First, if you decide to go hiking alone, make sure to tell others where you're going and when you'll be back. Second, there are some light items you should carry: waterproof matches, fire starter, multi-use camp tool, whistle, compass, and emergency blanket (which is actually smaller than a wallet). More important, bring a full water bottle and an extra supply of granola bars.

If you think you're lost, don't panic. Others know the direction you were headed in and will start looking for you. Look around to see if anything—such as an unusual tree or a mountain peak— looks familiar, or if there are tracks you can follow. If nothing looks familiar or if it's getting dark, stay put and let others find you. Try to stay warm and maximize your food and water supplies. If you have your matches and fire starter, build a safe fire. If you hear someone, use your whistle to signal your location. Three short blasts is the universal distress call.

7 Ecology of the Camp

Aside from ensuring your own personal safety, your main responsibility as a camper is to leave your campsite in better condition than you found it. Campgrounds receive thousands of visitors each year, so it's the campers' job to minimize their impact on their surroundings.

Pooping in the Woods

If your campground doesn't have toilet facilities, ask park officials about waste disposal. Aside from its obvious offensiveness, human waste presents a health hazard. It contains intestinal bacteria and sometimes disease organisms that can make other campers sick.

Digging tool

Learn how to dispose of waste correctly. Dig a hole that is six to eight inches deep, where decomposing microorganisms can thrive. Keep the sod lid intact and set it aside. Pile the rest of the dirt next to it. Then you're ready to do your business!

Afterward, scoop the dirt into the hole. Use a stick to mix the waste into the dirt to hasten decomposition. Replace the sod lid and camouflage the hole as much as possible. Don't bury used

Enjoy the view, and preserve it for others.

toilet paper. Always take it with you. You may have heard that
to be ecologically kind you should use leaves instead of toilet
paper. Don't. You might infect your anus with dirty leaves or,
even worse, poison ivy or poison oak.

Where do you dig a hole? You must keep a distance of at
least 200 feet or seventy paces from natural water sources.
Avoid places where your waste may be transported by flood-
ing, runoff, or groundwater seepage. Keep your waste from
being found by people and wildlife; keep a distance of 200 feet
from campsites, trails, and food sources for animals.

Some campers even carry their own portable latrines,
available at outdoor suppliers. They empty the waste at
approved dump sites. Never throw human waste in a trash
can or Dumpster, because this is also a health hazard and is
illegal in most states. Park officials can tell you where such
waste is collected.

Urinate in places where the urine can evaporate quickly, such as on rocks and in sunny areas. Keep at least 200 feet from natural water sources.

Washing Up

When you finish with your hole or with urination, wash up. Don't risk getting sick by preparing food with contaminated hands. But how do you do this without contaminating the environment with your soap suds? Soap has chemicals that kill fish and plants. Leave soap at home, but use wet hand wipes from any grocery store. Remember, the fragrance-free kind won't attract bears and bees.

You can also use waterless hand cleansers. Look for a brand that contains zinc pyrithione, an antimicrobial agent. Rub the cleanser on your hands, wipe off the excess, and you're clean.

As for your hair and body, you can wash them when you're back home. If you must do it outdoors, apply all the rules for protecting water sources and keep your use of soap to a minimum. Never soap up and then jump in a stream to rinse off. Save the rinsing water and reuse it to clean your pots and pans.

Try washing dishes with wet sand or coarse soil instead of soap. The sand works like a scouring pad, so food scrapes off easily.

Breaking Camp

If you have been organized and environmentally conscious while camping, it will make breaking camp easy. If you made a fire, make certain the fire pit is cold. Do not scatter leftover firewood among the trees. Make a neat stack next to the fire pit. Check for litter, which you will take with you, then cover the depression with fresh dirt or gravel.

Pick up all garbage around the camp, especially plastic or other non-biodegradable items. Do not leave behind any food, which may attract animals to the camp. Do not bury garbage; bears will find it and dig it up. If you burn garbage, you still have to take the unburned parts with you.

Take only pictures; leave only footprints!

After you take down your tent, scatter natural debris over the ground where it stood. When your camp looks as if you were never there, then you're finished. As Woodsy Owl of the Forest Service says, "Lend a Hand—Care for the Land!"

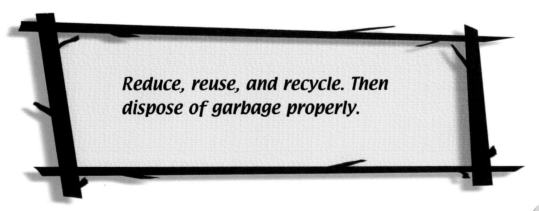

Reduce, reuse, and recycle. Then dispose of garbage properly.

Glossary

Biodegradable
Something that can decompose or decay and be absorbed by the environment.

Conservation
The protection of natural resources such as trees, rivers, and minerals.

Cryptosporidium
A parasite found in untreated water that causes fever, vomiting, fatigue, and diarrhea.

Decompose
To rot or decay.

Dehydration
When the body, an organ, or a bodily part loses too much water.

Flammable
Able to be set on fire easily.

Giardia
A parasite found in untreated water that causes stomach cramps, diarrhea, and vomiting.

Heatstroke
A serious illness caused by exposure to excessive heat.

Hypothermia
A serious illness caused by exposure to excessive cold.

Outfitter

A person or store that furnishes equipment for special purposes, such as camping.

Parasite

An animal or plant that lives on or in another animal or plant.

Parka

A warm fur or cloth jacket with a hood.

Pitch

To set up, as in "to pitch a tent."

Synthetic

A material made by people that is not found in nature.

Tarp

A waterproof piece of material used to protect things from moisture; also called a tarpaulin.

Resources

In the United States

American Camping Association (ACA)
5000 State Road 67 North
Martinsville, IN 46151
(765) 342-8456
Web site: http://www.acacamps.org

American Red Cross
Attn: Public Inquiry Office
11th Floor
1621 North Kent Street
Arlington, VA 22209
Web site: http://www.redcross.org

National Park Service (NPS)
1849 C Street NW
Washington, DC 20240
(202) 208-6843
Web site: http://www.nps.gov

National Recreation Reservation Service™ (NRRS)
(877) 444-6777
Web site: http://www.ReserveUSA.com

Sierra Club
85 Second Street, Second Floor
San Francisco, CA 94105
(415) 977-5500
Web site: http://www.sierraclub.org

USDA Forest Service
Sydney R. Yates Federal Building
201 14th Street, S.W.
Washington, DC 20024
(202) 205-1657
Web site: www.fs.fed.us

In Canada
Canadian Forest Service (CFS)
580 Booth Street, 8th Floor
Ottawa, ON K1A 0E4
(613) 947-7341
Web site: http://www.nrcan.gc.ca/cfs

Canadian Parks and Wilderness Society (CPWS)
880 Wellington Street, Suite 506
Ottawa, ON K1R 6K7
(800) 333-WILD
(613) 569-7226
Web site: http://www.cpaws.org

For Further Reading

American Camping Associates Staff. *Guide to American Camping Association Accredited Camps.* Martinsville, IN: American Camping Association, 1998.

Griffin, Steven A. *The Camping Sourcebook: Your One-Stop Resource for Everything to Feed Your Camping Habit.* Old Saybrook, CT: Globe Pequot, 1997.

Logue, Victoria. *Camping in the 90's: Tips, Techniques & Secrets.* Birmingham, AL: Menasha Ridge Press, 1995.

Logue, Victoria, and Frank Logue. *Kids Outdoors: The Totally Nonboring Backcountry Skills Guide.* New York: McGraw-Hill, 1996.

Love, Douglas. *The Ultimate Camp-Out Party Book.* New York: William Morrow, 1997.

Rutter, Michael. *Camping Made Easy: A Manual for Beginners with Tips for the Experienced.* Old Saybrook, CT: Globe Pequot, 1997.

Woodall's Publishing Staff. *Woodall's Camping Guide: Canada, 1998.* Lake Forest, IL: Woodall, 1997.

Index

Credits

About the Author

Jacqueline Ching is a New York-based writer and editor. Her work for The Rosen Publishing Group includes three titles in the Missions of California series.

Photo Credits

Cover photo © Alan Kearney/FPG; p. 5 © John Clausen/Mountain Stock; pp. 7, 29 © VCG/FPG; p. 8 © Ramond Gehman/Corbis; p. 9 © Lanny Johnson/Mountain Stock; p. 9 © Kevin Schafer/Corbis; p. 10, 33, 57 © Corbis; pp. 12, 23, 33, 38, 40, 41, 43, 51, 52 © Superstock; p. 17 © Telegraph Colour Library/FPG; p. 19 © Hank deVre/Mountain Stock; p. 25 © Roger Ressmeyer/CORBIS; p. 27 © Stephen Simpson/FPG; p. 31 © Walter Smith/FPG; p. 35 © David Whitten/Mountain Stock; p. 37 © Alan Kearney/FPG; p. 45 © Cheyenne Rouse/Mountain Stock; p. 49 © Kevin Lahey/Moutain Stock; p. 50 © Anne Marie Weber/Mountain Stock; p. 55 © Alissa Crandall/Corbis.

Series Design and Layout

Oliver H. Rosenberg

Series Editors

Erica Smith and Annie Leah Sommers